Lisp Interpreter in Rust

Vishal Patil

Contents

Introduction

Welcome to **lisp-rs**, a hands-on guide to implementing a bare-bones Lisp interpreter in Rust! This project implements a simplified version of Scheme, a Lisp dialect, and takes you on a journey to explore the inner workings of an interpreter. Whether you're a seasoned Rustacean or a programming language enthusiast, this book strives to offer a clear path to understanding how interpreters are constructed and how Rust enhances this process.

Why Lisp?

Lisp, with its minimalist yet powerful design, enjoys a legendary status among programming languages. Since its inception, it has served as a foundation for countless academic endeavors and practical programming paradigms. Its simplicity, rooted in S-expressions, dynamic typing, and homoiconicity (code as data), makes it an ideal teaching tool for understanding language implementation.

By focusing on a subset of Scheme, we aim to ensure that the process remains approachable, while still tackling the most critical features that make Lisp a joy to work with.

Why Rust?

Rust is often heralded for its memory safety, performance, and modern language features. For those building interpreters, it provides powerful tools such as:

- **Enums and Pattern Matching**: Perfect for representing and manipulating Lisp datatypes like lists, atoms, and symbols in a clean and expressive way.

- **Smart Pointers**: Allow safe, flexible memory management for tasks that traditionally require garbage collection.

- **Error Handling**: Rust's Result and Option types simplify dealing with parsing or runtime errors.

The purpose of this book is not only to explore how a Lisp interpreter can be built but also to showcase how Rust's strengths make it an enjoyable experience to implement complex systems like language interpreters.

Who Is This Book For?

This book assumes basic familiarity with Rust and some comfort with programming concepts. If you've written a program or two in Rust, you're already well-prepared! However, to follow this project smoothly, a basic understanding of these computer science and Rust concepts will be beneficial:

1. Computer Science Concepts

- **Lists**: As fundamental as they are in Lisp, you'll understand and manipulate them frequently.

- **Recursion**: Integral to the evaluation process in Lisps, recursion is at the core of how interpreters process expressions.

2. Rust Knowledge

- **Enums and Pattern Matching**: Used for structuring Lisp datatypes and evaluation logic.
- **Smart Pointers**: To handle shared data elegantly (e.g., Rc, RefCell).
- **Error Handling**: To gracefully handle parsing and runtime errors in the interpreter.

If these concepts feel unfamiliar, don't worry! Along the way, we'll offer context and examples to make sure you're not left behind.

Book Structure

The book is structured into three incremental parts to introduce concepts step-by-step, ensuring that the Lisp interpreter grows organically in complexity while remaining easy to understand.

Part I: Laying the Foundation

We implement the core of the interpreter, covering:

- Essential **data types**: integers, floats, booleans and strings.

- Basic **expressions**: variable definitions, assignments, conditions, and functions.

- Core **keywords**: define, if—else, and lambda.

- A minimal **REPL** (Read-Eval-Print Loop) to interactively execute Lisp code.

By the end of Part I, you'll be able to run simple Lisp programs like:

```
(define fact
  (lambda (n)
    (if (< n 1)
        1
        (* n (fact (- n 1))))))

(fact 5)
```

Part II: Building Functionality

We expand the interpreter to support:

- Core Lisp functions such as **list, car, cdr, cons, null?, length,** and constructs like **cond, begin,** and **let**

- Functional constructs: **map, filter,** and **reduce**.

This part bridges the gap between a basic interpreter and a more expressive Lisp dialect that demonstrates Lisp's practicality and extensibility.

Part III: Advanced Lisp Features

In this phase, we dive deeper and implement:

- **Tail Call Optimization**: Ensuring efficient recursion for functional programming needs.
- **Closures**: Enabling functions to capture and carry their environments.

By the end of Part III, you'll have a deeper appreciation for the advanced constructs that make Lisp a powerful tool, along with the satisfaction of implementing these from scratch.

Code Walkthrough and Tools

Each component of the interpreter is broken into four core modules:

- **Lexer**: Tokenizes Lisp code (**lexer.rs**).
- **Parser**: Converts tokens into abstract syntax trees (**parser.rs**).
- **Evaluator**: Implements the core evaluation rules of Lisp (**eval.rs**).
- **REPL**: A command-line interface to dynamically execute Lisp code (**main.rs**).

All critical code snippets are included in the text. However, to enhance your understanding, you're encouraged to download the code and follow along directly:

```
git clone https://github.com/vishpat/lisp-rs
cd lisp-rs
git checkout 2.0.1
```

You can run the REPL with the following command:

```
cargo run --features="build-binary"
```

And test the code with:

```
cargo test
```

What Will You Learn?

By the end of this book, you'll have a fully functioning Lisp interpreter implemented in Rust. You'll understand:

- How Lisp interpreters evaluate expressions.
- How Rust's ecosystem and type system aid in implementing parsers and evaluators.
- Common patterns used in language construction (e.g., managing environments, handling recursive evaluation, building REPLs).

But most importantly, this project invites you into Lisp's fascinating world and shows how enjoyable and rewarding it can be to create programming tools from the ground up.

Let's get started on this exciting journey! Lisp and Rust are both incredible tools. By combining their power, you'll not only grow your skills but also gain a deeper appreciation for language design and implementation.

Part I

What is Lisp?

Lisp is one of the oldest programming languages; due to its elegance and simplicity, it is a natural fit for teaching language implementation concepts. Lisp interpreters revolve around a concise, expressive syntax: S-expressions, a seamless integration of code and data, and a reliance on a core set of powerful primitives. In this chapter, we'll explore the major steps involved in implementing a Lisp interpreter, specifically focusing on tokenization, parse tree generation, evaluation and REPL (read-eval-print-loop), while showcasing how Lisp's simplicity makes these steps tractable.

Lisp is an abbreviation for **List Processor**. Every Lisp program is simply a **list expression.** The elements of this list can either be:

- Atomic values, such as an integer, float, boolean or a string.

- Another list expression (nested lists).

Thus, a Lisp program is a **recursive list expression**, as shown below:

9

$$(a\ (b\ c\ d\ (e\ (f\ g))))$$

```
list1:  (a                          )
list2:       (b c d                 )
list3:              (e          )
list4:                    (f g)
```

In the example above:

- The outermost list (a ...) contains the atomic symbol a and another list (b c d (e (f g))).

- Nested lists include:

  - (b c d ...)
  - (e ...)
  - (f g)

This recursive structure is what makes Lisp unique.

How Does a Lisp Interpreter Work?

A Lisp interpreter is a software program designed to:

- Parse the textual representation of a Lisp program.

- Create an **in-memory, list-based recursive data structure**.

Once the Lisp program is represented as a data structure, interpreting it involves recursively **evaluating these lists.**

10

This simplicity makes Lisp both elegant and powerful.

The interpreting process is broken down into **three main phases**:

Tokenization
The interpreter converts the text of the Lisp program into a **stream of tokens.** Tokens are the smallest building blocks of the program, such as symbols, parentheses, or literals.

Parsing
The token stream is converted into an **in-memory recursive list-based data structure.**

Evaluation
The program is executed by recursively walking through the in-memory recursive list, applying functions to their respective arguments, and producing the final result.

Tokenization: Breaking Down the S-Expressions

Lisp programs are written as symbolic expressions, or **S-expressions**, which nest deeply and are enclosed in parentheses. This makes Lisp's syntax strikingly simple compared to other languages, such as Python or C++, and tokenization relatively straightforward.

The Purpose of Tokenization in Lisp

In Lisp, tokenization performs the basic task of extracting meaningful units (tokens) from the input program so that the interpreter can process them. Typical tokens in Lisp include:

- **Parentheses**, which define the structure of expressions.
- **Atoms**, which are either symbols (e.g., x, +, my−fn) or literals like numbers (42, 3.14), booleans (#t,#f) and strings (`"hello"`).
- **Whitespace**, which separates tokens but is otherwise ignored.

How Lisp Tokenization Works

- Read the raw source code as a string.
- Scan the string character by character, grouping characters into tokens while respecting Lisp's syntax. This involves:
    - Identifying parentheses as structural tokens.
    - Distinguishing between atoms and literals.
    - Ignoring whitespace.
- Output a flat list of tokens.

Example

Given the Lisp program:

```
(+ 1 (* 2 3))
```

The tokenizer outputs the following list of tokens:

```
["(", "+", "1", "(", "*", "2", "3", ")", ")"]
```

Parse Tree Generation: Building the S-Expression

Once the program is tokenized, the next step is to **parse** the tokens into a tree structure. In Lisp, the parse tree is essentially the program itself, represented as a nested collection of lists (Lisp's fundamental data structure). These lists are the S-expressions that make Lisp both dynamic and easy to manipulate.

The Purpose of Parsing in Lisp

The goal of parsing in Lisp is to reconstruct the hierarchical structure of the program that is implicitly encoded in the parentheses. Parsing organizes the tokens into nested lists so that the interpreter can process the program's logic.

How Parsing Works

- Start with the token list produced in the previous step.
- Recursively group tokens into nested lists:
    - Open parentheses (() indicate the start of a new sub-list.
    - Close parentheses ()) mark the end of the current sublist.
    - Atoms and literals are added as elements of the current list.
- Generate a nested representation of the program.

Example

For the token list from earlier:

```
[ "(", "+", "1", "(", "*", "2", "3", ")", ")" ]
```

The parser produces the following parse tree (or equivalently, this S-expression):

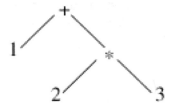

Evaluation: Traversing and Executing the S-Expression

S-expressions in Lisp don't just represent code—they *are* the code. The final step in the interpreter is **evaluation**, where these nested lists are traversed and executed. At this stage, the actual computation or logic in the program takes place.

The Purpose of Evaluation in Lisp

Evaluation resolves the meaning of the S-expression by: 1. Interpreting symbols (e.g., variables or functions). 2. Applying functions to arguments. 3. Producing results or side effects (e.g., modifying state or printing output).

How Evaluation Works

Evaluation in Lisp is recursive and follows a few simple rules:

- If the input is an **atom**:

- If it's a literal (e.g., a number, boolean or string), re-turn it as-is.
- If it's a symbol, look it up in the **environment** (i.e., the symbol table) to retrieve its value.
- If the input is a **list**:
    - Evaluate the first element of the list (the operator).
    - Evaluate the remaining elements of the list (the arguments).
    - Apply the operator to the arguments.

Example

For the S-expression:

```
(+ 1 (* 2 3))
```

Evaluation proceeds as follows:

- Evaluate the * sub-expression first:
    - Look up *, the multiplication operator.
    - Compute (* 2 3)=> 6
- Replace the * sub-expression with its result:
    - (+ 1 6)
- Evaluate the + expression:
    - Compute (+ 1 6)=> 7

The final result is 7.

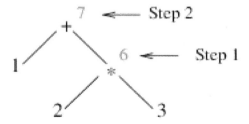

Interactive Evaluation: The REPL

A key feature of many Lisp implementations is the **REPL**, which stands for:

Read: Read a Lisp expression from input.

Evaluate: Compute the result by interpreting the expression.

Print: Output the result to the user.

Loop: Wait for the next user input.

For example, in a REPL:

```
> (+ 2 3)
5
> (list 1 2 3)
(1 2 3)
```

Next Steps

The following chapters in this book will walk you through the process of implementing a Lisp interpreter. The interpreting process is broken down into three phases:

Lexing: Converting the Lisp program text into a stream of tokens.

Parsing: Converting the stream of tokens into an in-memory recursive list data structure.

Evaluation: Walking the in-memory recursive list and producing the final result.

In addition, the final chapter in Part I will implement a simple **REPL** to evaluate the Lisp program.

Lexer

A **tokenizer** (aka lexer) is a fundamental component of an interpreter. It's responsible for breaking down the raw program text into a sequence of meaningful units called tokens. This chapter delves into the implementation of a tokenizer in Rust for our Lisp interpreter.

Tokens: Building Blocks of the Program

In our Lisp interpreter, every meaningful piece of text becomes a **token**. These tokens form the building blocks of our program.

In Rust, we define our tokens using the following enum:

```
#[derive(Debug, Clone, PartialEq)]
pub enum Token {
    Integer(i64),
    Symbol(String),
    LParen,
    RParen,
    Float(f64),
```

```
    String(String),
    BinaryOp(String),
    Keyword(String),
}
```

Tokenization Process

Tokenization is the process of splitting a program into meaningful units: tokens. Here's how it works:

1. **Split the Input**: Break the program into words.

2. **Generate Tokens**: Map each word into a Token using pattern matching.

For example, the following Lisp code:

```
(define sqr (* x x))
```

is tokenized to a vector

```
[
    Token::LParen, Token::Keyword("define"),
    Token::Symbol("sqr"),
    Token::LParen, Token::BinaryOp("*"),
    Token::Symbol("x"), Token::Symbol("x"),
    Token::RParen, Token::RParen
]
```

Visualized, the token vector looks like this:

20

(define sqr (* x x))

)
)
x
x
*
(
sqr
define
(

Vector of tokens

Tokenizer Implementation in Rust

Our tokenizer is built using Rust, following a modular approach.

1. Tokenizer Struct

The Tokenizer struct holds the program's state during tokenization:

```rust
struct Tokenizer<'a> {
    input: Chars<'a>,              // Char iterator of the
        program text.
    current_char: Option<char>, // Current char being
        processed.
    keywords: HashSet<&'a str>, //  Supported Lisp
        keywords.
    binary_ops: HashSet<char>,  //  Supported Binary
        operators.
}
```

2. Initialization

The **new** method initializes the tokenizer with the program text, along with predefined keywords and operators.

```rust
impl<'a> Tokenizer<'a> {
    pub fn new(input: &'a str) -> Self {
        let mut chars = input.chars();

        // HashSet of Keywords
        let keywords = ["define", "if", ...].into_iter().
            collect();
```

```
// HashSet of Binary Operators
let binary_ops = ['+', '-', ...].into_iter().collect
    ();

Tokenizer {
    input: chars,
    current_char: chars.next(),
    keywords,
    binary_ops,
}
}
```

3. Token Parsing

To convert the text into tokens, the tokenizer provides helper methods for different token types.

Next character

```
fn advance(&mut self) -> Option<char> {
  self.current_char = self.input.next();
  self.current_char
}
```

Whitespace Handling

```
fn eat_whitespace(&mut self) {
  while let Some(c) = self.current_char {
    if !c.is_whitespace() {
```

23

```rust
            break;
        }
        self.advance();
    }
}
```

Symbols

```rust
fn read_symbol(&mut self) -> String {
    let mut symbol = String::new();
    while let Some(c) = self.current_char {
        if c.is_whitespace() || c == '(' || c == ')' {
            break;
        }
        symbol.push(c);
        self.advance();
    }
    symbol
}
```

Numbers

```rust
fn read_number(&mut self) -> String {
    let mut number = String::new();
    while let Some(c) = self.current_char {
        if !c.is_numeric() && c != '.' {
            break;
        }
        number.push(c);
        self.advance();
    }
```

```
      number
}
```

Strings

```
fn read_string(&mut self) -> String {
    let mut string = String::new();
    self.advance();
    while let Some(c) = self.current_char {
        if c == '"' {
            self.advance();
            break;
        }
        string.push(c);
        self.advance();
    }
    string
}
```

Main Token Parsing Logic

The **next_token** function processes the input and generates tokens:

```
pub fn next_token(&mut self) -> Option<Token> {
    self.eat_whitespace();

    match self.current_char? {
        '(' => {
            self.advance();
            Some(Token::LParen)
```

25

```
            }
            ')' => {
                self.advance();
                Some(Token::RParen)
            }
            '"' => Some(Token::String(self.read_string())),
            c if c.is_numeric() => {
                let val = self.read_number();
                if val.contains('.') {
                    Some(Token::Float(val.parse().unwrap()))
                } else {
                    Some(Token::Integer(val.parse().unwrap()))
                }
            }
            c if c.is_alphabetic() ||
                self.binary_ops.contains(&c) => {
                let sym = self.read_symbol();
                if self.keywords.contains(sym.as_str()) {
                    Some(Token::Keyword(sym))
                } else if self.binary_ops.contains(&sym.\
                chars().next().unwrap()) {
                    Some(Token::BinaryOp(sym))
                } else {
                    Some(Token::Symbol(sym))
                }
            }
            _ => None,
        }
    }
}
```

The **tokenize** function applies this tokenizer to the entire input:

```
pub fn tokenize(input: &str) -> Result<Vec<Token>,
```

```
                TokenError> {
    let mut tokenizer = Tokenizer::new(input);
    let mut tokens = Vec::new();
    while let Some(token) = tokenizer.next_token() {
        tokens.push(token);
    }

    Ok(tokens)
}
```

Testing the Tokenizer

Unit tests ensure the correctness of the tokenizer. Below are two test cases:

Testing Addition

```
#[test]
fn test_add() {
    let tokens = tokenize("(+ 1 2)").unwrap();
    assert_eq!(tokens, vec![
        Token::LParen,
        Token::BinaryOp("+".to_string()),
        Token::Integer(1),
        Token::Integer(2),
        Token::RParen,
    ]);
}
```

Testing Area of a Circle

```rust
#[test]
fn test_area_of_a_circle() {
  let program = "
    (
        (define r 10)
        (define pi 3.14)
        (* pi (* r r))
    )
  ";
  let tokens = tokenize(program).unwrap();
  assert_eq!(
      tokens,
      vec![
        Token::LParen,
        Token::LParen,
        Token::Keyword("define".to_string()),
        Token::Symbol("r".to_string()),
        Token::Integer(10),
        Token::RParen,
        Token::LParen,
        Token::Keyword("define".to_string()),
        Token::Symbol("pi".to_string()),
        Token::Integer(314),
        Token::RParen,
        Token::LParen,
        Token::BinaryOp("*".to_string()),
        Token::Symbol("pi".to_string()),
        Token::LParen,
        Token::BinaryOp("*".to_string()),
        Token::Symbol("r".to_string()),
        Token::Symbol("r".to_string()),
        Token::RParen,
        Token::RParen,
        Token::RParen
```

```
            ]
        );
}
```

Parser

The **parser** is an integral part of the Lisp interpreter. Its role is to translate the output of the **lexer** (a stream of tokens) into a **recursive structure** that represents the program's abstract syntax tree (AST). In the case of Lisp, this structure is typically a tree of nested **Lists** with elements such as symbols, integers, strings, or other sub-lists.

This chapter delves into the following topics:

- **Object Model**: The foundational data structure for representing Lisp objects.

- **Parser Implementation**: Converting tokens into Lisp objects.

Object Model

Before we can parse a Lisp program, we must define the objects that can make up its abstract syntax tree (AST). In our implementation, this is done using the Object enum in Rust. Each variant in the enum represents a possible data type in our Lisp dialect.

```rust
#[derive(Debug, Clone, PartialEq)]
pub enum Object {
    Void,
    Keyword(String),
    BinaryOp(String),
    Integer(i64),
    Float(f64),
    Bool(bool),
    String(String),
    Symbol(String),
    ListData(Vec<Object>),
    Lambda(Vec<String>, Vec<Object>),
    List(Rc<Vec<Object>>),
}
```

To make these objects easier to debug and interpret, the Object enum implements the **fmt::Display** trait:

```rust
impl fmt::Display for Object {
    fn fmt(&self, f: &mut fmt::Formatter) -> fmt::Result {
        match self {
            Object::Void => write!(f, "Void"),
            Object::Keyword(s) => write!(f, "{}", s),
            Object::BinaryOp(s) => write!(f, "{}", s),
            Object::Integer(n) => write!(f, "{}", n),
            Object::Float(n) => write!(f, "{}", n),
            Object::Bool(b) => write!(f, "{}", b),
            Object::Symbol(s) => write!(f, "{}", s),
            Object::String(s) => write!(f, "{}", s),
            Object::Lambda(params, body) => {
                write!(f, "Lambda(")?;
                for param in params {
                    write!(f, "{} ", param)?;
                }
```

```
            write!(f, ")")?;
            for expr in (*body).iter() {
              write!(f, " {}", expr)?;
            }
            Ok(())
          }
          Object::List(list) => {
            write!(f, "(")?;
            for (i, obj) in (*list).iter().enumerate() {
              if i > 0 {
                write!(f, " ")?;
              }
              write!(f, "{}", obj)?;
            }
            write!(f, ")")
          }
          Object::ListData(list) => {
            write!(f, "(")?;
            for (i, obj) in list.iter().enumerate() {
              if i > 0 {
                write!(f, " ")?;
              }
              write!(f, "{}", obj)?;
            }
            write!(f, ")")
          }
        }
      }
    }
  }
```

This implementation ensures that each object is formatted appropriately when printed during debugging or REPL interaction.

Parsing the Code

The parser's main task is to transform a vector of tokens (produced by the lexer) into a recursive list structure, which is the backbone of Lisp programs. Let's start by understanding how the parse function operates.

The `parse` Function

The primary entry point for the parser is the parse function. It takes a string containing the program as input, tokenizes it, and converts the tokens into an Object. This function handles errors gracefully by returning a Result.

```
pub fn parse(program: &str) -> Result<Object,
    ParseError> {
  let token_result = tokenize(program);
  if token_result.is_err() {
    return Err(ParseError {
      err: token_result.err().unwrap().to_string()
    });
  }

  let mut tokens = token_result.unwrap()\
        .into_iter().rev().collect::<Vec<_>>();
  let parsed_list = parse_list(&mut tokens)?;
  Ok(parsed_list)
}
```

The parser uses **parse_list** as a recursive helper function. This function operates on a stack of tokens (reversed for efficient pop operations) and produces a single List object.

Code Walkthrough

Parsing a List:

The parse_list function contains the logic to build a Lisp list.

- It expects a left parenthesis (Token::LParen) at the beginning.

- It iterates through the remaining tokens, either:

  - Parsing literals, such as numbers or symbols.

  - Recursively descending into sub-lists when encountering another left parenthesis.

  - Terminating when encountering a right parenthesis (Token::RParen).

Here's the core implementation:

```rust
fn parse_list(tokens: &mut Vec<Token>) ->
    Result<Object, ParseError> {

  let token = tokens.pop();
  if token != Some(Token::LParen) {
    return Err(ParseError { err:
    format!("Expected LParen, found {:?}", token) });
  }

  let mut list: Vec<Object> = Vec::new();
  while !tokens.is_empty() {
    let token = tokens.pop();
    if token.is_none() {
      return Err(ParseError
    { err: "Unexpected end of input".to_string() });
    }
```

```
    match token.unwrap() {
      Token::Integer(n) => list.push(Object::Integer(n))
          ,
      Token::Float(f) => list.push(Object::Float(f)),
      Token::String(s) => list.push(Object::String(s)),
      Token::Symbol(s) => list.push(Object::Symbol(s)),
      Token::LParen => {
        // Push back '(' and recurse
        tokens.push(Token::LParen);
        let sub_list = parse_list(tokens)?;
        list.push(sub_list);
      }
      Token::RParen => {
        return Ok(Object::List(Rc::new(list)));
      }
      _ => {
        return Err(ParseError { err:
      format!("Unexpected token {:?}", token) });
      }
    }
  }

  Err(ParseError { err: "Missing closing parenthesis".
      to_string() })
}
```

Testing

Testing the parser ensures that it behaves correctly for different inputs. The **test_add** and **test_area_of_a_circle** functions provide examples.

Example Test: Parsing a Basic Expression

```rust
#[test]
fn test_add() {
  let list = parse("(+ 1 2)").unwrap();
  assert_eq!(
   list,
   Object::List(Rc::new(vec![
    Object::BinaryOp("+".to_string()),
    Object::Integer(1),
    Object::Integer(2),
   ]))
  );
}
```

Example Test: Parsing a Nested Program

```rust
#[test]
fn test_area_of_a_circle() {
  let program = "(
                  (define r 10)
                  (define pi 3.14)
                  (* pi (* r r))
                )";
  let list = parse(program).unwrap();
assert_eq!(
      list,
      Object::List(Rc::new(vec![
        Object::List(Rc::new(vec![
          Object::Keyword("define".to_string()),
          Object::Symbol("r".to_string()),
          Object::Integer(10),
        ])),
        Object::List(Rc::new(vec![
          Object::Keyword("define".to_string()),
```

```rust
                Object::Symbol("pi".to_string()),
                Object::Float(3.14),
            ])),
            Object::List(Rc::new(vec![
                Object::BinaryOp("*".to_string()),
                Object::Symbol("pi".to_string()),
                Object::List(Rc::new(vec![
                    Object::BinaryOp("*".to_string()),
                    Object::Symbol("r".to_string()),
                    Object::Symbol("r".to_string()),
                ])),
            ])),
        ]))
    );
}
```

The Evaluator

The **evaluator** is the core of any Lisp interpreter. This component takes the parsed representation of a Lisp program, evaluates it, and produces the final result. In this chapter, we'll dive deep into how the evaluator is implemented in Rust. By the end of the chapter a fully functional evaluator will be implemented that will enable you to write some basic programs in Lisp.

What Does the Evaluator Do?

At a high level, the evaluator processes the **Abstract Syntax Tree (AST)** generated by the parser. It recursively evaluates each node of the AST, handling primitive data types, special forms like define and if, and user-defined and built-in functions.

Evaluation is driven by several key operations:

- **Atomic Objects**:
    - Booleans, integers, floats, strings, and symbols are evaluated directly based on their type or through environment lookups (for symbols).

- **Special Forms**:

    - Certain keywords like define, **if**, cond and lambda are evaluated specially, as they define variables, evaluate conditions, or create functions, respectively.

- **Environment**:

    - Environments are hierarchical structures that map variable names to their corresponding values.

    - The global environment is the root, containing predefined constants and functions.

    - Nested environments are created during function calls or expressions requiring their own scope, allowing for lexical scoping.

Implementation

The evaluator is implemented in the eval.rs module. We'll now discuss its major components and their functionality.

Note: This chapter will use the branch **2.0.1** to explain the evaluator. The evaluator implementation in the main branch is advanced as it implements tail call optimization and will be covered in the third part of the book.

eval_obj

The eval_obj function is the starting point for evaluation. It delegates different types of objects to their respective evaluation strategies:

```
fn eval_obj(
```

```
    obj: &Object,
    env: &mut Rc<RefCell<Env>>,
) -> Result<Object, String> {
    match obj {
        Object::Void => Ok(Object::Void),
        Object::Bool(_) => Ok(obj.clone()),
        Object::Integer(n) => Ok(Object::Integer(*n)),
        Object::Float(f) => Ok(Object::Float(*f)),
        Object::ListData(list) => eval_list_data(list, env),
        Object::String(_) => Ok(obj.clone()),
        Object::Symbol(s) => eval_symbol(s, env),
        Object::Lambda(_, _) => Ok(Object::Void),
        Object::List(list) => eval_list(list, env),
        _ => Err(format!("Invalid object: {:?}", obj)),
    }
}
```

- Atomic Objects: Booleans, strings, integers, and floats are directly returned without further processing.

- Symbols: Symbols represent variable names or function calls. The *eval_symbol* function retrieves the value associated with the symbol in the current environment

- Lists: Lists are evaluated with the *eval_list* and *eval_list_data* functions. The eval_list function evaluates function calls, while eval_list_data is used create a list of objects.

env

Before understanding the *eval_symbol* function, it is essential to understand the design of how variables are implemented

41

for the Lisp interpreter.

The variables are just *string* labels assigned to objects, and they are created using the **define** keyword. Note a variable can represent an atomic value or a function object.

```
(
  (define x 1)
  (define sqr (lambda (r) (* r r)))
)
```

This Lisp code defines (or creates) two variables, *x*, and *sqr*, representing an integer and function object respectively. Also, the scope of these variables lies within the *list object* that they are defined under. This is achieved by storing the mapping from the variable names (strings) to the objects in a map-like data structure called *Env*.

```rust
// env.rs
pub struct Env {
    parent: Option<Rc<RefCell<Env>>>,
    vars: HashMap<String, Object>,
}

impl Env {
    pub fn new() -> Self {
        Default::default()
    }

    pub fn update(&mut self, data: Rc<RefCell<Self>>) {
        self.vars.extend(
            data
                .borrow()
```

```
            .vars
            .iter()
            .map(|(k, v)| (k.clone(), v.clone()))),
    );
}

pub fn extend(parent: Rc<RefCell<Self>>) -> Env {
    Env {
        vars: HashMap::new(),
        parent: Some(parent),
    }
}

pub fn get(&self, name: &str) -> Option<Object> {
    match self.vars.get(name) {
        Some(value) => Some(value.clone()),
        None => self
            .parent
            .as_ref()
            .and_then(|o| o.borrow().get(name).clone()),
    }
}

pub fn set(&mut self, name: &str, val: Object) {
    self.vars.insert(name.to_string(), val);
}
}
```

The interpreter creates an instance of *Env* at the program's start to store the global variable definitions. In addition, for every function call, the interpreter creates a new instance of env and uses the new instance to evaluate the function call. This latest instance of env contains the function parameters and a *back* pointer to the *parent* env instance from where the function is called. This back pointer is used to resolve symbols not associated with the function parameters, as shown below with an example.

```
(
   (define m 10)
   (define n 12)
   (define K 100)

   (define func1
      (lambda (x) (+ x K)))

   (define func2
      (lambda (x) (− x K)))

   (func1 m)
   (func2 n)
)
```

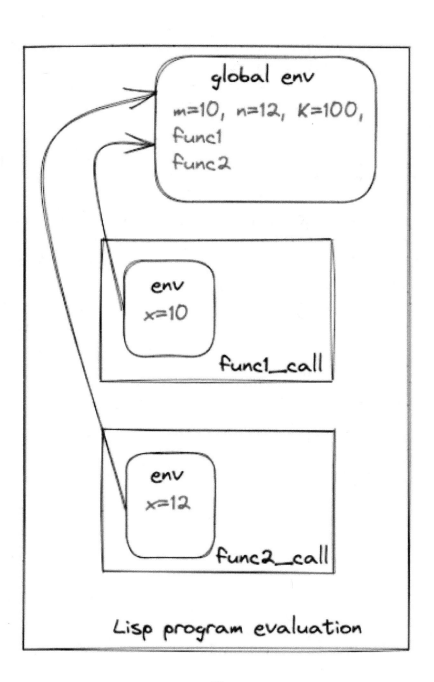

45

In the above example, the value for symbol K in the body of the functions **func1** and **func2** is resolved by the parent env using the *parent* back pointer. This concept will become more apparent as we go through the implementation.

eval_symbol

The job of *eval_symbol* is to look up the object bound to the symbol. This is done by looking up the symbol in the passed *env* variable or any of its parent *env* until the *root env* of the program.

```
// eval.rs

fn eval_symbol(
    s: &str,
    env: &mut Rc<RefCell<Env>>,
) -> Result<Object, String> {
    let val = match s {
        ....
        _ => env.borrow_mut().get(s),
    };

    if val.is_none() {
        return Err(format!("Unbound symbol: {}", s));
    }

    Ok(val.unwrap().clone())
}
```

eval_list

The *eval_list* function recursively evaluates a list expression and is implemented as shown below.

```
let head = &list[0];
match head {
    Object::Keyword(_) => eval_keyword(list, env),
    Object::BinaryOp(_) => eval_binary_op(list, env),
    Object::Symbol(s) => eval_function_call(s, list, env
        ),
    _ => Err(format!("Invalid list op: {:?}", list))
}
```

The function first peeks at the head of the list and if it encounters a keyword, a binary operator or a symbol object as the first element of the list, it processes the list according to the object that gets matched. The following sections explain how the list is evaluated depending on the type of first object.

Variables

```
(define sqr (lambda (x) (* x x)))
```

If the head of the list in the *eval_list* function matches the *define* keyword, the *eval_define* function gets called (via eval_keyword). The *eval_define* function calls *eval_obj* on the third list argument and assigns the evaluated object value to the symbol defined by the second argument. The symbol and the evaluated object value are stored in the current *env*.

47

```
fn eval_define(list: &Vec<Object>, env: &mut Rc<RefCell<
    Env>>)
            -> Result<Object, String> {
    let sym = match &list[1] {
        Object::Symbol(s) => s.clone(),

        . . . .

        _ => return Err(format!("Invalid define")),
    };
    let val = eval_obj(&list[2], env)?;
    env.borrow_mut().set(&sym, val);
    Ok(Object::Void)
}
```

In the example above, the symbol *sqr* and the function object representing the lambda will be stored in the current *env*. Once the function *sqr* has been defined, any latter code can access the corresponding function object by looking up the symbol *sqr* in *env*.

Binary Operations

```
(+ x y)
```

If the head of the list in the *eval_list* function matches a binary operator, the *eval_binary_op* function gets called. The *eval_binary_op* function calls the *eval_obj* on the second and third element of the list and performs the appropriate binary operation on the evaluated values depending on the binary operator.

```
fn eval_binary_op(
    list: &[Object],
    env: &mut Rc<RefCell<Env>>,
) -> Result<Object, String> {
    if list.len() != 3 {
        return Err(
            "Invalid number of arguments for infix operator"
                .to_string(),
        );
    }
    let operator = list[0].clone();
    let left = &eval_obj(&list[1].clone(), env)?;
    let right = &eval_obj(&list[2].clone(), env)?;
    match operator {
        Object::BinaryOp(s) => match s.as_str() {
            "+" => match (left, right) {
                (Object::Integer(l), Object::Integer(r)) => {
                    Ok(Object::Integer(l + r))
                }
                (Object::Float(l), Object::Float(r)) => {
                    Ok(Object::Float(l + r))
                }
                (Object::Integer(l), Object::Float(r)) => {
                    Ok(Object::Float(*l as f64 + r))
                }
                (Object::Float(l), Object::Integer(r)) => {
                    Ok(Object::Float(l + *r as f64))
                }
                (Object::String(l), Object::String(r)) => {
                    Ok(Object::String(l.to_owned() + r))
                }
                _ => Err(format!(
                    "Invalid types for + operator {} {}",
                    left, right
                )),
```

49

```
        },
      ....
}
```

If expression

```
(if (> x y) x y)
```

If the head of the list in the *eval_list* function matches the *if* keyword, the *eval_if* function is called (via eval_keyword). The *eval_if* function calls *eval_obj* on the second element of the list and, depending upon whether the evaluated value is true or false, calls the eval_obj on either the third or fourth element of the list and returns the value.

```
fn eval_if(list: &Vec<Object>, env: &mut Rc<RefCell<Env
    >>)
-> Result<Object, String> {

  let cond_obj = eval_obj(&list[1], env)?;
  let cond = match cond_obj {
    Object::Bool(b) => b,
    _ => return Err(format!("Condition must
               be a boolean")),
  };

  if cond == true {
    return eval_obj(&list[2], env);
  } else {
    return eval_obj(&list[3], env);
  }
```

```
}
```

Lambda

```
(lambda (x y) (* x y))
```

If the head of the list in the *eval_list* function matches the *lambda* keyword, the *eval_function_definition* function gets called (via eval_keyword). The *eval_function_definition* function evaluates the second element of the list as a vector of *parameter names* (string symbols).

```
fn eval_function_definition(list: &Vec<Object>) ->
    Result<Object, String> {
  let params = match &list[1] {
    Object::List(list) => {
      let mut params = Vec::new();
      for param in list {
        match param {
          Object::Symbol(s) => params.push(s.clone()),
          _ => return Err(format!("Invalid lambda
            parameter")),
        }
      }
      params
    }
    _ => return Err(format!("Invalid lambda")),
  };
```

The *eval_function_definition* function then clones the third list element as the function body.

51

```
let body = match &list[2] {
  Object::List(list) => list.clone(),
  _ => return Err(format!("Invalid lambda")),
};
```

The evaluated parameters and body are returned as the *lambda* object.

```
Ok(Object::Lambda(params, body.to_vec()))
```

For example, in the case of the following lambda.

```
(define max
  (lambda (x y)
    (if (> x y)
        x
        y)))
```

The *x* and *y* parameter symbols will be stored in the *params* vector as strings "x" and "y". The recursive List Object representing the *if* expression will be held in the *body* vector.

Function Call

```
(find_max a b c)
```

Suppose the head of the list is a Symbol object, and it does not match any of the keywords mentioned above or binary operators. The interpreter assumes that the Symbol object maps to a Lambda (function object). An example of the function call in Lisp is shown above. To evaluate such list the *eval_function_call* function is called. This function first performs the lookup for the function object using the function name, *find_max* in the case of this example. It returns an error if no object is found.

```
fn eval_function_call(
    s: &str,
    list: &Vec<Object>,
    env: &mut Rc<RefCell<Env>>,
) -> Result<Object, String> {

    let lamdba = env.borrow_mut().get(s);
    if lamdba.is_none() {
        return Err(format!("Unbound symbol: {}", s));
    }
```

A new *env* object is created if the function object is found. This new *env* object has a *back* pointer to the parent *env* object. This is required to get the values of the variables not defined in the function's scope. The new *env* object is local to the function execution scope.

```
let mut new_env = Rc::new(
            RefCell::new(
            Env::extend(env.clone())));
```

The next step in evaluating the function call requires preparing the function parameters. This is done by iterating over the remainder of the list and evaluating each parameter. The

parameter name and the evaluated object are set in the new
env object.

```
for (i, param) in params.iter().enumerate() {
    let val = eval_obj(&list[i + 1], env)?;
    new_env.borrow_mut().set(param, val);
}
```

Finally, the function body is evaluated by passing the new_env,
which contains the parameters to the function.

```
return eval_obj(&Object::List(body), &mut new_env);
```

This completes the execution of the function call by the interpreter.

Testing

The evaluator code can be unit tested, as shown below. In
each test case, we create a global env object. The env object
and the program text are then passed to the *eval* function to
get the program result. The generated result object is then
compared with a hand-built expected result object for verifi-
cation.

```
#[test]
fn test_simple_add() {
    let mut env = Rc::new(RefCell::new(Env::new()));
    let result = eval("(+ 1 2)", &mut env).unwrap();
    assert_eq!(result, Object::Integer(3));
```

```rust
}

#[test]
fn test_area_of_a_circle() {
    let mut env = Rc::new(RefCell::new(Env::new()));
    let program = "(
                    (define r 10)
                    (define pi 314)
                    (* pi (* r r))
                 )";
    let result = eval(program, &mut env).unwrap();
    assert_eq!(
        result,
        Object::List(vec![Object::Integer((314 * 10 * 10) as
            i64)])
    );
}

#[test]
fn test_sqr_function() {
    let mut env = Rc::new(RefCell::new(Env::new()));
    let program = "(
                    (define sqr
                      (lambda (r) (* r r)))

                    (sqr 10)
                 )";
    let result = eval(program, &mut env).unwrap();
    assert_eq!(
        result,
        Object::List(vec![Object::Integer((10 * 10) as i64)
            ])
    );
}
```

```rust
#[test]
fn test_fibonacci() {
    let mut env = Rc::new(RefCell::new(Env::new()));
    let program = "
        (
            (define fib
                (lambda (n)
                    (if (< n 2)
                        1
                        (+ (fib (- n 1)) (fib (- n 2))))))

            (fib 10)
        )
    ";

    let result = eval(program, &mut env).unwrap();
    assert_eq!(result,
        Object::List(vec![Object::Integer((89) as i64)]));
}

#[test]
fn test_factorial() {
    let mut env = Rc::new(RefCell::new(Env::new()));
    let program = "
        (
            (define fact
                (lambda (n)
                    (if (< n 1)
                        1
                        (* n (fact (- n 1))))))

            (fact 5)
        )
    ";
```

```
let result = eval(program, &mut env).unwrap();
assert_eq!(result,
    Object::List(vec![Object::Integer((120) as i64)]));
}
```

Conclusion

The evaluator is the backbone of a Lisp interpreter. By under-standing its architecture and adapting it with new function-ality, we can extend the interpreter to support increasingly complex programs, pushing the boundaries of what can be achieved in Lisp.

REPL

The REPL is the CLI (Command Line) interface that a user uses to interact with the interpreter. The user types in a program line and hits *Enter*. The interpreter immediately evaluates the line of the program and produces the result. The **main.rs** Rust module implements the REPL for the interpreter.

Implementation

The REPL is relatively straightforward to implement compared to other components of the interpreter. The functionality is implemented with the help of the linefeed crate.

The REPL first creates an instance of *env* to hold the global variables for the interpreter.

```
let mut env = Rc::new(RefCell::new(env::Env::new()));
```

The REPL is a simple while loop that takes one line as an input from the user, evaluates it, and prints out the evaluated object. The REPL is terminated if the user enters the **exit** keyword.

```rust
while let ReadResult::Input(input) =
              reader.read_line().unwrap() {

    if input.eq("exit") {
        break;
    }
    let val = eval::eval(input.as_ref(), &mut env)?;
    match val {
      Object::Void => {}
      Object::Integer(n) => println!("{}", n),
      Object::Bool(b) => println!("{}", b),
      Object::Symbol(s) => println!("{}", s),
      Object::Lambda(params, body) => {
        println!("Lambda(");
        for param in params {
            println!("{} ", param);
        }
        println!(")");
        for expr in body {
            println!(" {}", expr);
        }
      }
      _ => println!("{}", val), // prints all other
          objects
    }
}
```

The *fmt::Display* crate implemented by the object enables the printing of the object values to the console.

Part II

Advanced Features

Now that the basic interpreter is working, we shall focus on adding some more *advanced* features to it. Please note that *advanced* does not mean more complicated. If you understand this book so far, you have already understood the most challenging part of the interpreter. What follows next should be pretty straightforward for you to understand.

The following new features will be added next to the interpreter.

Constants

- #t (boolean true)
- #f (boolean false)
- #nil (null)

Data Types

- list

Functions

- list

- car
- cdr
- cons
- cond
- null?
- length
- begin
- let

Functional Constructs

Using the above functions following functional constructs will be implemented in Lisp

- map
- filter
- reduce

Constants

Constants such **#t** (boolean true), **#f** (boolean false), and **nil** (null) can be added to the interpreter by evaluating them directly in the eval_symbol function, without defining them with the define keyword, as follows

```
fn eval_symbol(s: &str, env: &mut Rc<RefCell<Env>>)
   -> Result<Object, String> {

  let val = match s {
    "#t" => return Ok(Object::Bool(true)),
    "#f" => return Ok(Object::Bool(false)),
    "nil" => return Ok(Object::Void),
    _ => env.borrow_mut().get(s),
  };

  if val.is_none() {
    return Err(format!("Unbound symbol: {}", s));
  }

  Ok(val.unwrap().clone())
}
```

These can then be utilized in a Lisp program as follows.

```
(
  (define on-beach #t)

  (define clothing
    (if on-beach
      "flip-flops"
      "shoes"))
)
```

The if expression evaluates the *on-beach* variable to *true*, and thus, the variable clothing is assigned the value "flip-flops" in the above expression.

Functions

This chapter will discuss the implementation of the core Lisp functions in the evaluator.

list

In Lisp, the **list** function is a core utility that creates a new list from the given set of arguments, for example.

```
(define list−of−cities (list "Raleigh" "Durham" "Chapel
    Hill"))
(define list−of−integers (list 1 2 3 4))
(define mixed−list (list 1 2 3.0 "4"))
```

No changes are required to the Lexer or the Parser to add support for the list data type. However, a new **ListData** object needs to be added to the object model to represent the list of objects.

```
pub enum Object {
    ...
    + ListData(Vec<Object>),
```

```
    }
```

The list object creation is part of the evaluation process in the *eval_keyword* function. When this function encounters the **list** keyword as the first element of the list, it calls the *eval_list_data* function.

```
let head = &list[0];
match head {
    Object::Keyword(s) => match s.as_str() {
        ...
+       "list" => eval_list_data(&list, env),
        ...
    }
```

The *eval_list_data* function creates the List object by creating a new vector and adding the **evaluated** list elements.

```
fn eval_list_data(
    list: &[Object],
    env: &mut Rc<RefCell<Env>>,
) -> Result<Object, String> {

    let mut new_list = Vec::new();

    for obj in list[1..].iter() {
        new_list.push(eval_obj(obj, env)?);
    }

    Ok(Object::ListData(new_list))
}
```

Finally, the *ListData* object is returned as it is when it is encountered in the *eval_obj* function.

```
Object::ListData(l) => Ok(Object::ListData(l.to_vec()))
```

car

In Lisp, the **car** function returns the first element (also known as the head) of the list.

```
> (define list-of-cities (list "Raleigh" "Durham" "
    Chapel Hill"))
> (car list-of-cities)
> Raleigh
```

The **car** functionality is implemented in the evaluator using the **eval_car** function as follows.

```
fn eval_car(
   list: &[Object],
   env: &mut Rc<RefCell<Env>>,
) -> Result<Object, String> {

   let l = eval_obj(&list[1], env)?;

   match l {
     Object::ListData(list) => Ok(list[0].clone()),
     _ => Err(format!("{} is not a list", l)),
   }

}
```

This function evaluates the parameter (*list[1]*) (which is the list), passed to the *car* function and if the evaluated object is a list, returns the copy of the first element of the list. If the first parameter does not evaluate to a list, it returns an error.

cdr

The **cdr** function in Lisp returns a new list containing all elements of the original list except the first one (the head). This is often referred to as the "tail" of the list.

```
> (define list−of−cities (list "Raleigh" "Durham" "
    Chapel Hill"))
> (cdr list−of−cities)
> ("Durham" "Chapel Hill")
```

The **cdr** functionality is implemented by the **eval_cdr** function as follows.

```
fn eval_cdr(
   list: &[Object],
   env: &mut Rc<RefCell<Env>>,
) −> Result<Object, String> {
   let l = eval_obj(&list[1], env)?;
   let mut new_list = vec![];
   match l {
     Object::ListData(list) => {
        for obj in list[1..].iter() {
           new_list.push(obj.clone());
```

```
            }
        Ok(Object::ListData(new_list))
    }
    _ => Err(format!("{} is not a list", l)),
    }
}
```

Similar to *car*, this function evaluates it's argument and checks if it results in a *ListData* object. If it does, it creates a new list containing all elements of the original list starting from the second element, and returns it as a new *ListData* object. If the argument isn't a list, it returns an error.

cons

The cons function constructs a new list by adding an element to the beginning of an existing list. It's how you build up lists from individual elements.

```
> (cons "New York" (list "Raleigh" "Durham"))
> ("New York" "Raleigh" "Durham")
```

The eval_cons function implements the cons functionality:

```
fn eval_cons(
    list: &[Object],
    env: &mut Rc<RefCell<Env>>,
) -> Result<Object, String> {
    if list.len() != 3 {
        return Err(
```

```
        "Invalid number of arguments for cons".to_string()
              ,
      );
    }

    let head = eval_obj(&list[1], env)?;
    let tail = eval_obj(&list[2], env)?;

    match tail {
        Object::ListData(mut l) => {
            l.insert(0, head);
            Ok(Object::ListData(l))
        }
        _ => Err(format!("{} is not a list", tail)),
    }
}
```

This function expects two arguments. It evaluates both the head (element to add) and the tail (the existing list). If the tail is a list, it creates a new list with head inserted at the beginning and returns it. If the tail is not a list, it returns an error.

null?

The null? function is a predicate (a function that returns a boolean) that checks if a list is empty or not. It returns #t if a list is empty, and #f otherwise.

```
> (null? (list))
> #t
```

```
> (null? (list 1 2 3))
> #f
```

The **eval_is_null** function implements the **null?** function in the evaluator

```
fn eval_is_null(
    list: &[Object],
    env: &mut Rc<RefCell<Env>>,
) -> Result<Object, String> {

    let obj = eval_obj(&list[1], env)?;

    match obj {
        Object::List(list) => Ok(Object::Bool(list.is_empty
            ())),
        Object::ListData(list) => {
            Ok(Object::Bool(list.is_empty()))
        }
        _ => Err(format!("{} is not a list", obj)),
    }
}
```

This function first evaluates the given argument, and if the re-sulting value is a list (*Object::List* or *Object::ListData*), it then uses the *is_empty()* method to determine if the list is empty and returns #t if it is empty and #f otherwise. If the argument is not a list, it returns an error.

length

The length function returns the number of elements in the list.

```
> (length (list "Raleigh" "Durham" "Chapel Hill"))
> 3
```

The **eval_length** function implements the **length** function in the evaluator as follows.

```
fn eval_length(
    list: &[Object],
    env: &mut Rc<RefCell<Env>>,
) -> Result<Object, String> {

    let obj = eval_obj(&list[1], env)?;

    match obj {
        Object::List(list) => {
            Ok(Object::Integer(list.len() as i64))
        }
        Object::ListData(list) => {
            Ok(Object::Integer(list.len() as i64))
        }
        _ => Err(format!("{} is not a list", obj)),
    }
}
```

This function evaluates the given argument. If the argument evaluates to a list (either Object::List or Object::ListData), the function returns the number of elements in the list as an Integer. If it is not a list it returns an error.

74

cond

The cond special form provides a general way to create conditional expressions, similar to an **if—else** structure. Each clause in a cond form consists of a test and a body. The clauses are checked in order; when a test evaluates to true (anything other than #f and #nil), the body of the clause is executed and the result is returned. If the keyword else is used as a condition, it will be executed if no other condition is met.

```
(cond ((> x 10) "x is greater than 10")
      ((< x 10) "x is less than 10")
      (else "x is equal to 10"))
```

The **eval_cond** function implements the **cond** function in the evaluator as follows.

```
fn eval_cond(
  list: &[Object],
  env: &mut Rc<RefCell<Env>>,
) -> Result<Object, String> {
  if list.len() < 2 {
    return Err(
      "Invalid number of arguments for cond".to_string()
      ,
    );
  }

  for l in list[1..].iter() {
    match l {
      Object::List(list) => {
        if list.len() != 2 {
          return Err(format!(
```

75

```rust
                "Invalid cond clause {:?}",
                list
            ));
        }

        if list[0] == Object::Keyword(
            "else".to_string()) {
          return eval_else(list, env);
        }

        let cond = eval_obj(&list[0], env)?;
        let cond_val = match cond {
          Object::Bool(b) => b,
          _ => {
            return Err(format!(
              "Condition must be a boolean {:?}",
              cond
            ))
          }
        };
        if cond_val {
          return eval_obj(&list[1], env);
        }
      }
      _ => return Err("Invalid cond clause".to_string())
                ,
    }
  }

  Err("No cond clause matched".to_string())
}
```

This function iterates through the cond clauses, evaluates the conditional expression, and if it is true then evaluates the body of the clause. If the keyword else is encountered then the else body is executed. If none of the clauses match an error is returned.

```
fn eval_else(
    list: &[Object],
    env: &mut Rc<RefCell<Env>>,
) -> Result<Object, String> {
    if list.len() != 2 {
        return Err(format!(
            "Invalid number of arguments for else {:?}",
            list
        ));
    }

    eval_obj(&list[1], env)
}
```

begin

The **begin** special form allows a sequence of expressions to be evaluated one after the other, and returns the result of the last expression. It's a way to group operations. It creates a new scope for variables defined in the block.

```
(begin
    (define x 10)
    (define y 20)
    (+ x y)
)
```

The above begin block returns a value of 30.

The **eval_begin** function implements the **begin** function in the evaluator as follows.

```
fn eval_begin(
    list: &[Object],
    env: &mut Rc<RefCell<Env>>,
) -> Result<Object, String> {
    let mut result = Object::Void;
    let mut new_env =
        Rc::new(RefCell::new(Env::extend(env.clone())));

    for obj in list[1..].iter() {
        result = eval_obj(obj, &mut new_env)?;
    }
    Ok(result)
}
```

let

The **let** special form creates local bindings for variables within a given scope. It is useful for avoiding name conflicts when you need temporary variables. Like begin, it creates a new scope, but this scope is only for the let variables and the let body.

```
(let ((x 10) (y 20))
    (+ x y)
)
```

78

The **eval_let** function implements the **let** function in the evaluator as follows.

```
fn eval_let(
  list: &[Object],
  env: &mut Rc<RefCell<Env>>,
) -> Result<Object, String> {
  let mut result = Object::Void;
  let bindings_env = Rc::new(RefCell::new(Env::new()));

  if list.len() < 3 {
    return Err(
      "Invalid number of arguments for let".to_string(),
    );
  }

  let bindings = match list[1].clone() {
    Object::List(bindings) => bindings,
    _ => {
      return Err("Invalid bindings for let".to_string())
    }
  };

  for binding in bindings.iter() {
    let binding = match binding {
      Object::List(binding) => binding,
      _ => {
        return Err("Invalid binding for let".to_string()
          )
      }
    };

    if binding.len() != 2 {
      return Err("Invalid binding for let".to_string());
    }
```

```
    let name = match binding[0].clone() {
      Object::Symbol(name) => name,
      _ => {
        return Err("Invalid binding for let".to_string()
          )
      }
    };

    let value = eval_obj(&binding[1], env)?;
    bindings_env.borrow_mut().set(name.as_str(), value);
  }

  println!("let arguments {:?}", bindings_env);
  let mut new_env =
    Rc::new(RefCell::new(Env::extend(env.clone())));
  new_env.borrow_mut().update(bindings_env);

  for obj in list[2..].iter() {
    result = eval_obj(obj, &mut new_env)?;
  }
  Ok(result)
}
```

This function first extracts the variable bindings, then creates a new local scope and binds each of the variables to its value by evaluating each of the variables assigned values in the environment. Then it extends the given environment with the local scope and evaluates the remaining expressions in the let block in that environment and returns the result of the last expression.

Conclusion

With these functions implemented, the Lisp interpreter now has basic list manipulation capabilities, conditional execution, and local scoping, allowing you to write more complex and structured programs. The ability to work with lists, manipulate them, and control the flow of execution are fundamental to any Lisp implementation.

Functional Constructs

This chapter will explore several powerful functional programming constructs implemented as Lisp functions: map, filter, and reduce. These functions are foundational building blocks in functional programming, providing concise and expressive ways to manipulate lists.

Map

The map function applies a given function to each element of a list and returns a new list containing the results. It's used for transforming each element of a list in some way. The core idea is to perform an operation on each item, producing a new collection of transformed items.

Implementation

Here's the Lisp code that implements map:

```
(begin
    (define (map f l)
        (if (null? l)
```

```
            (list)
            (cons (f (car l)) (map f (cdr l)))))
   (map (lambda (x) (* x x)) (list 1 2 3 4 5))
)
```

Explanation

1. Function Definition:

```
(define (map f l) ...)
```

This defines a function named map that takes two arguments:
f (a function to apply) and l (the input list).

2. Base Case:

```
(if (null? l)
    (list)
    ...)
```

The if statement checks if the input list l is empty using the
null? function. If the list is empty, map returns an empty list
((list)). This is the base case for the recursion.

3. Recursive Step:

```
(cons (f (car l)) (map f (cdr l)))
```

If the list is not empty, the cons function does the following:

- (car l) extracts the first element of the list.

- (f (car l)) applies the function f to the first element.
- (map f (cdr l)) recursively calls map with the same function f and the rest of the list ((cdr l)). This applies f to all remaining elements and builds a new result list.
- The cons function constructs a new list by adding the result of applying f to the first element, to the head of the result of the recursive call with the remaining elements.

4. **Example Usage:**

```
(map (lambda (x) (* x x)) (list 1 2 3 4 5))
```

This demonstrates the map function. It squares each number in the list (list 1 2 3 4 5).

- (lambda (x)(* x x)) is an anonymous function that squares its input value
- The list (list 1 2 3 4 5) is passed as the second argument to map function.

This will result in a new list containing (1 4 9 16 25).

Summary

The map function demonstrates a common pattern in functional programming: processing each item in a collection with a function to create a new transformed collection.

Filter

The filter function selects elements from a list that satisfy a given predicate (a function that returns a boolean). It returns a new list containing only those elements that pass the test.

Implementation

Here's the Lisp code that implements filter:

```
(begin
    (define (filter f l)
        (if (null? l)
            (list)
            (if (f (car l))
                (cons (car l) (filter f (cdr l)))
                (filter f (cdr l))))))
    (filter (lambda (x) (> x 2)) (list 1 2 3 4 5))
)
```

Explanation

1. Function Definition:

```
(define (filter f l) ...)
```

This defines a function named filter that takes two arguments: f (a predicate function) and l (the input list).

2. Base Case:

```
(if (null? l)
    (list)
    ...)
```

If the input list l is empty, filter returns an empty list, as there are no elements to filter.

86

3. **Recursive Step:**

```
(if (f (car l))
    (cons (car l) (filter f (cdr l)))
    (filter f (cdr l)))
```

- (car l) extracts the first element of the list.
- (f (car l)) applies the predicate f to the first element of the list.
- If it evaluates to #t, the first element is included in the filtered list by prepending to the result of recursively filtering the remaining list.
- If it evaluates to #f, the first element is discarded, and the filter function recursively filters only the remaining list by calling filter with the same predicate function and the cdr of the list.

4. **Example Usage:**

```
(filter (lambda (x) (> x 2)) (list 1 2 3 4 5))
```

This demonstrates filter by creating a new list that contains only the numbers greater than 2 from the list (list 1 2 3 4 5).

- (lambda (x)(> x 2)) is an anonymous function that returns #t if its input is greater than 2 and #f otherwise.
- The list (list 1 2 3 4 5) is passed as the second argument.

This will result in a new list containing (3 4 5).

Summary

The filter function demonstrates how to conditionally include elements from a collection based on a given predicate.

Reduce

The reduce function is a higher-order function that applies a binary operation cumulatively to the items of a list, effectively "reducing" the list to a single value. It's a core concept in functional programming, often used to aggregate or combine list elements. The key idea is to successively combine the elements of the list using the given binary function.

Implementation

Here is the Lisp code for reduce:

```
(begin
    (define (reduce f l)
        (if (null? l)
            (list)
            (if (null? (cdr l))
                (car l)
                (f (car l) (reduce f (cdr l))))))
    (reduce (lambda (x y) (+ x y)) (list 1 2 3 4 5))
)
```

Explanation

1. **Function Definition:**

88

```
(define (reduce f l) ...)
```

This defines a function named reduce that takes two arguments: f (a binary function) and l (the input list).

2. Base Cases:

```
(if (null? l)
     (list)
  ...)
```

If the input list l is empty, reduce returns an empty list as there
is nothing to reduce. This is where the current implementation deviates from some implementations, as it returns a list
instead of an error.

```
(if (null? (cdr l))
     (car l)
  ...)
```

If the list only has one element, then return the first element
in the list.

3. Recursive Step:

```
(f (car l) (reduce f (cdr l)))
```

- (car l) extracts the first element of the list.

- (reduce f (cdr l)) recursively reduces the list after removing the first element by calling the reduce function with the same function f and the cdr of the list.
- (f (car l) (reduce f (cdr l))) the function f is applied to the first element and the result of recursively reducing the rest of the list.

4. **Example Usage:**

```
(reduce (lambda (x y) (+ x y)) (list 1 2 3 4 5))
```

This sums all the elements in the list (list 1 2 3 4 5).

- (lambda (x y)(+ x y)) is an anonymous function that takes two arguments and adds them together. The arguments are two values being reduced.
- (list 1 2 3 4 5) is the list that will be reduced.

The reduction happens as follows:

- 1 + (2 + (3 + (4 + 5))) = 15

Summary

The reduce function demonstrates how a binary function can be used to combine the elements of a collection into a single value.

Conclusion

These functional constructs—map, filter, and reduce—provide a powerful, concise, and composable approach to data manipulation. By understanding these functions and how they can be used, you can elevate your Lisp programming skills and write more elegant and efficient code. These functions form the basis of more complex functional algorithms and are a staple of functional programming.

Part III

Stack Overflow

Before we understand how tail call optimization is implemented, it is essential to know why it is needed. Consider the following Lisp program, which computes the sum of the first n integers using a *tail-recursive* approach.

```
(define sum-n
  (lambda (n a)
    (if (= n 0) a
      (sum-n (- n 1) (+ n a)))))

(sum-n 100 0)
```

This program works fine for small values of **n**; however, if you run this program with large values for *n*, the interpreter will crash with a *StackOverflow* error.

Let's look at how our interpreter (version 2.0.1) evaluates the above function call to understand why it would crash for large values of n. Our current implementation for evaluation looks like the following.

```
// eval.rs - version 2.0.1
```

```
fn eval_obj(obj: &Object, env: &mut Rc<RefCell<Env>>)
    -> Result<Object, String>
{
    match obj {
        ...
        Object::List(list) => eval_list(list, env),
        ...
    }
}
```

```
//  eval.rs - version 2.0.1

fn eval_if(list: &Vec<Object>, env: &mut Rc<RefCell<Env
    >>)
    -> Result<Object, String>
{
    ...
    if cond == true {
        return eval_obj(&list[2], env);
    } else {
        return eval_obj(&list[3], env);
    }
}
```

When the function call for *sum-n* is evaluated, the *eval_obj*
function calls the *eval_list* function, which in turn calls the
eval_if (via *eval_keyword*), which ends up calling the *eval_obj*
function again. In the case of a recursive function call, this
program flow is repeated multiple times. Thus recursive function calls create multiple stack frames. As the number of re-
cursions increases, so do the needed stack frames. Since the

96

Operating System limits the stack size for a process, the inter-preter eventually hits this limit. At this point, the Operating System terminates the interpreter with a stack overflow error.

Tail Call Optimization

The stack overflow problem mentioned in the previous chapter seriously limits the usage of *Tail Recursive* functions. Tail recursive functions are functions in which the last expression to be evaluated for a function is a call to itself. *Tail recursive algorithms* are often used to solve problems elegantly.

Since many problems can be solved elegantly using *Tail Recursive Algorithms*, it is essential to eliminate the stack overflow problem. *Tail Call Optimization* is a technique that will help us overcome this problem by eliminating the interpreter's recursive *eval_obj* calls.

The current *evaluator* call stack for implementing an *if* expression looks as follows

```
// Pseudo code
// if expression evaluation using recursion
// Here obj represents an if expression

eval_obj(obj)
  ...
  eval_if
    eval_obj(next_obj)
```

Similarly, the *evaluator* call stack for implementing the *function call* looks as follows.

```
// Pseudo code
// function call evaluation using recursion
// Here obj represents a function call expression

eval_obj(obj)
  ...
    eval_function_call
      eval_obj(next_obj)
```

If you look closely, in both cases, the *eval_obj* is the last expression which is the cause of the recursion.

Now for a moment, let's assume Rust had support for a *goto* statement. Let us also believe that the interpreter stores a reference to the current object that it is evaluating in a global variable called *current_obj*. We could modify the above call stack to use goto and eliminate recursive calls to *eval_obj* with these assumptions.

```
// Pseudo code
// if evaluation using tail call optimization

global current_obj

eval_obj(obj_in)
  current_obj = obj_in
  EVAL:  ...
        ...
      eval_if
        current_obj = next_obj
```

```
        goto EVAL
```

```
// Pseudo code
// function call evaluation using tail call optimization

global current_obj

eval_obj(obj_in)
  current_obj = obj_in
  EVAL: ...

      ...
    eval_function_call
        current_obj = next_obj
        goto eval
```

Modifying the program flow to evaluate an object by jumping back to the start of the *eval_obj* function is crucial for implementing tail call optimization. This hack eliminates a function call, thereby avoiding a stackframe allocation. Note, this optimization is possible only because the *eval_obj* call was the last expression in **if** and **function call** evaluations.

Since Rust does not have support for goto and goto is a wrong design choice, we will implement this functionality using a Rust *loop* in the *eval_obj* function. This will be explained in detail in the following sections.

Implementation

The implementation for tail call optimization requires changes only in the evaluator portion of the interpreter.

Code

```
git clone https://github.com/vishpat/lisp-rs
git checkout 2.0.2
```

Evaluator

For the implementation of tail call optimization, the core of the evaluator changes is in the *eval_obj* function.

```
fn eval_obj(obj: &Object, env: &mut Rc<RefCell<Env>>) ->
    Result<Object, String> {
    let mut current_obj = Box::new(obj.clone());
    let mut current_env = env.clone();
    ...
}
```

Compared to the previous versions, the first change to the *eval_obj* function is that the object to be evaluated is now *Boxed*, and the variable *current_obj* that owns the Boxed object is mutable. This is required because the object which will be evaluated will change in the loop as part of the evaluation process. The Box allows the current_obj to be mutable and be changed during the evaluation process.

To implement the *goto* logic explained earlier, the evaluator processing is done inside a Rust *loop*. Although the evaluator loop could look overwhelming, it's pretty straightforward. If you look closely at its parts, you should be already familiar with most of the code. The big difference between the *eval_obj* function for tail call optimization from its predecessors is that the *If* and *function call* expression evaluation are inlined instead of being encapsulated in separate functions. This is to change the object (*current_obj*) being evaluated without recursively calling the *eval_obj* function. The loop replaces the function calls with jumps, just like goto was doing in the previous chapter.

```
loop {
  match *current_obj {
    Object::List(list) => {
      let head = &list[0];
      match head {
        Object::BinaryOp(_op) => {
          return eval_binary_op(&list, &mut current_env)
              ;
        }
        Object::Keyword(_keyword) => {
          if _keyword == "if" {
            .....
          }
        }

        Object::Symbol(s) => {
          ...
        }
        ...
      }
    }

    Object::Symbol(s) => {
      return eval_symbol(&s, &mut current_env);
    }
    Object::Void => return Ok(Object::Void),
```

```
        Object::Lambda(_params, _body) => return Ok(Object::
            Void),
        Object::Bool(_) => return Ok(obj.clone()),
        Object::Integer(n) => return Ok(Object::Integer(n)),
        Object::Float(n) => return Ok(Object::Float(n)),
        Object::String(s) => return Ok(Object::String(s.
            to_string())),
        Object::ListData(l) => return Ok(Object::ListData(l.
            to_vec())),
        _ => return Err(format!("Invalid object: {:?}", obj)
            ),
    }
}
```

The two aspects that are different from the previous evaluator are how the evaluator handles the *if* and the *function call* expressions. Both of these will be explained next.

If expression

The if expression evaluation happens as part of evaluating a list if the head of the list matches the *If* Object.

```
if _keyword == "if" {
    if list.len() != 4 {
        return Err(format!("Invalid number of arguments
            for if statement"));
    }

    let cond_obj = eval_obj(&list[1], &mut current_env)?;
    let cond = match cond_obj {
        Object::Bool(b) => b,
        _ => return Err(format!("Condition must be a
```

```
        boolean")),
    };

    if cond == true {
        current_obj = Box::new(list[2].clone());
    } else {
        current_obj = Box::new(list[3].clone());
    }
    continue;
}
```

As before evaluator evaluates the condition object for the *if*
expression and, depending on whether it evaluates to true or
false, updates the *current_obj* to the second or the third list
object and then continues the loop. This mechanism thus pre-
vents calling the *eval_obj* again, thereby avoiding a recursion.
The rest of the eval_obj loop will continue evaluating the up-
dated current_obj.

Function Call

As part of list evaluation, if the head of the list matches the
Symbol object, the evaluator assumes the list represents a
function call, the head of the list being the function name.

```
Object::Symbol(s) => {
    let lamdba = current_env.borrow_mut().get(s);
    if lamdba.is_none() {
        return Err(format!("Unbound function: {}", s));
    }

    let func = lamdba.unwrap();
    match func {
```

```
Object::Lambda(params, body) => {
    let new_env =
        Rc::new(RefCell::new(Env::extend(current_env.
            clone())));

    for (i, param) in params.iter().enumerate() {
        let val = eval_obj(&list[i + 1], &mut
            current_env)?;
        new_env.borrow_mut().set(param, val);
    }
    current_obj = Box::new(Object::List(body));
    current_env = new_env.clone();
    continue;
}
_ => return Err(format!("Not a lambda: {}", s)),
    }
}
```

Most function call evaluation is the same as in Part I, except instead of calling *eval_obj* on the function *body* and the *new_env*, the *current_obj* and the *current_env* are set to these values, and we continue evaluating the function call in the *eval_obj* loop.

Testing

The most fun way to test the tail call optimization feature is to fire up the REPL and run a tail recursive program against the different versions of the interpreter for high input values. For example, here is a tail recursive function to calculate the sum of integers up to *n*.

```
(define sum-n
  (lambda (n a)
    (if (= n 0) a
      (sum-n (- n 1) (+ n a)))))

(sum-n 100 0)
```

Try out this program for the different versions of the interpreter. The interpreter without the tail call optimization will crash with stack overflow errors for large values (on my machine for values greater than 2000), while the interpreter with the tail call optimization won't.

Following are some test cases for tail recursive functions that work with the interpreter.

Fibonacci generator

```
#[test]
fn test_tail_recursive_fibonacci()
{
    let mut env = Rc::new(RefCell::new(Env::new()));
    let program = "
        (
            (define fib
              (lambda (n a b)
                (if (= n 0) a
                  (if (= n 1) b
                    (fib (- n 1) b (+ a b))))))

            (fib 10 0 1)
        )
    ";
```

```
    let result = eval(program, &mut env).unwrap();
    assert_eq!(result,
      Object::List(vec![Object::Integer((55) as i64)]));
}
```

Factorial

```
#[test]
fn test_tail_recursive_factorial()
{
  let mut env = Rc::new(RefCell::new(Env::new()));
  let program = "
      (
          (define fact
              (lambda (n a)
                (if (= n 1) a
                  (fact (- n 1) (* n a))))))

          (fact 10 1)
      )
  ";

  let result = eval(program, &mut env).unwrap();
  assert_eq!(result,
      Object::List(vec![Object::Integer((3628800) as i64
        )]));
}
```

Closures

Closures enable a function (lambda) to capture the environment they are defined in. This means that the function will have access to the variables that were in scope when the function was created. Here is an example of how the closure will look in our interpreter.

```
(define add-n
  (lambda (n)
    (lambda (a) (+ n a))))

  (define add-3 (add-n 3))
  (define integers (list 1 2 3 4 5))

  (map add-3 integers)
```

The add-n lambda takes an integer *n* as its input and returns a new lambda with the integer *n* captured in it. In the above example, the add-3 lambda has the integer value of 3 caught in it because it was the value of n when add-n was called. The *map* expression then uses this lambda to add 3 to all values in the *integer* list.

109

Evaluator

The changes to add support for closures are limited to just the evaluator.

Object

The first step is to modify the *lambda* object to store a reference to the environment in which it is defined.

```
pub enum Object {
...
-   Lambda(Vec<String>, Rc<Vec<Object>>),
+   Lambda(Vec<String>, Rc<Vec<Object>>, Rc<RefCell<Env
       >>),
...
}
```

Function Definition

The *eval_function_definition*, which creates the lambda object, will be modified to take a new parameter *env*. The *env* parameter refers to the environment in which the lambda is defined. The *env* parameter is then passed to the lambda object as shown below.

```
fn eval_function_definition(
    list: &Vec<Object>,
    env: &mut Rc<RefCell<Env>>,
) -> Result<Object, String> {
    ...
```

```
      Ok(Object::Lambda(params, Rc::new(body.to_vec()), env.
          clone()))
}
```

Function Evaluation

The function evaluation in the *eval_obj* will be changed to capture the function env instead of extending the current env.
The captured environment is called a closure.

```
// eval_obj

- let new_env = Rc::new(RefCell::new(
-         Env::extend(current_env.clone())));

+ let new_env = Rc::new(RefCell::new(
+         Env::extend(func_env.clone())));
```

This will make the environment in which the function was defined available while evaluating the function call. With the new
environment, the function will have access to the variables defined when the function was created and the local variables
that are created when the function is called. With these simple changes, the interpreter will have support for closures.

Testing

```
#[test]
fn test_closure1() {
    let mut env = Rc::new(RefCell::new(Env::new()));
```

```rust
    let program = "
      (
        (define add-n
           (lambda (n)
               (lambda (a) (+ n a)))))
        (define add-5 (add-n 5))
        (add-5 10)
      )
    ";

    let result = eval(program, &mut env).unwrap();
    assert_eq!(
        result,
        Object::List(vec![Object::Integer((15) as i64)])
    );
}
```

Looking Ahead

Congratulations on reaching this point! You've journeyed through the intricacies of implementing a Lisp interpreter using the Rust programming language, gaining a deep understanding of both Lisp and Rust. But the journey doesn't have to end here. In fact, you're now standing at the threshold of an even more exciting adventure - the world of compiler construction.

In my second book, "LLVM API with Rust", we delve into the depths of using the LLVM API with Rust. LLVM, or Low Level Virtual Machine, is a library that is used to construct, optimize and produce intermediate and/or binary machine code. It forms the backbone of many modern language compilers, including Rust itself. By learning LLVM, you're equipping yourself with the knowledge used by professional compiler developers worldwide.

Moreover, the journey from interpreter to compiler is a logical and rewarding progression. While interpreters execute programs directly, compilers take a step further by translating program code into machine code, which can be executed more efficiently. This process involves several fascinating stages, including parsing, semantic analysis, optimization, and code generation. All these stages offer a wealth of learning opportunities and the chance to deepen your understanding of programming languages.

To aid your learning journey, I've created an open-source GitHub project that implements a Lisp compiler (scheme-rs) using the ideas from these books. This project serves as a practical guide, showing you how the concepts explained in the books can be applied to a real-world project. It's a living example of how a compiler can be built from scratch using Rust and LLVM.

I strongly encourage you to take this next step. Not only will it reinforce and expand upon what you've learned about Lisp and Rust, but it will also open new horizons in your understanding of how programming languages work under the hood.

Remember, every expert was once a beginner who took the first step. You've already taken several by making it this far. Keep going, and soon you'll find yourself in the company of those who not only use programming languages but also create them.

Happy coding!